FAMOUS CHILDHOODS

Wolfgang Amadeus
MOZART

Barrie Carson Turner

Chrysalis Children's Books

First published in the UK in 2003 by

Chrysalis Children's Books
64 Brewery Road, London N7 9NT

Copyright © Chrysalis Books PLC 2003
Text by Barrie Carson Turner

ISBN 184138 6952

British Library Cataloguing in Publication Data for this
book is available from the British Library.

A BELITHA BOOK

Editorial Manager: Joyce Bentley
Senior Editor: Sarah Nunn
Picture Researcher: Jenny Barlow

Produced by
Tall Tree Ltd
Editor: Jon Richards
Designer: Ed Simkins
Consultant: Yvonne Dix

Printed in China

10 9 8 7 6 5 4 3 2 1

PICTURE CREDITS

All reasonable efforts have been made to trace the relevant
copyright holders of the images contained within this book.
If we were unable to reach you, please contact Chrysalis Books.

B = bottom; *C* = centre; *L* = left; *R* = right; *T* = top.
Cover *background* The Art Archive/Biblioteca Nazionale Marciana Venice/Dagli Orti *front*
The Art Archive/Mozarteum Salzburg/Dagli Orti (A) *back* AKG London/Paris, Musée du
Louvre **1** Hulton Archive **2** AKG London/Paris, Musée du Louvre **4** The Art
Archive/Mozarteum Salzburg/The Art Archive **5** *T* The Art Archive/Mozarteum
Salzburg/Dagli Orti (A) *B* AKG London **6** The Art Archive/Mozarteum Salzburg/Dagli
Orti (A) **7** *T* AKG London/Heiner Heine *B* AKG London **8** AKG London/Erich Lessing
9 *L* AKG London/Residenzmuseum, Munich *R* AKG London **10** AKG
London/Kunsthistoriches Museum, Vienna **10-11** (see cover *front*) **11** AKG London/Erich
Lessing/Schloss Schoenbrunn, Vienna **12** (see **1**) **13** *T* AKG London/Erich Lessing/Paris,
Musée du Louvre *B* The Art Archive/Bibliotheque des Arts Decoratifs Paris/Dagli Orti
14 AKG London/Versailles Museum **15** *T* (see **2**) *B* Hulton Archive **16** AKG
London/Versailles Museum **17** *T* Mary Evans Picture Library *B* The Art
Archive/Historiches Museum (Museen der Stadt Wien) Vienna/Dagli Orti **18** Mary Evans
Picture Library **19** *T* AKG London/Amsterdam Rijksmuseum *B* AKG London/Versailles
Museum **20** AKG London **21** *L* and *R* AKG London **22** AKG London/Erich
Lessing/Historical Museum of the City of Vienna **23** *T* AKG London/Erich Lessing/Alte
Pinakothek, Munich *B* AKG London/Dresden, Staatliches Kupferstichkabinett **24** AKG
London/Erich Lessing/Mozart Museum der Stiftung Mozarteum, Salzburg **25** *T* AKG
London/Weimar, Geothe-Nationalmuseum *B* The Art Archive/Museo Bibliografico
Musicale Bologna/Dagli Orti (A) **26** (see cover *back*) **27** *T* The Art Archive/Musée du
Chateau de Versailles/Dagli Orti *B* AKG London/Museum Carolino Augusteum, Salzburg
28 Hulton Archive **28-29** *background* AKG London/Mozart Museum der Stiftung
Mozarteum, Salzburg **29** AKG London/Heiner Heine **30** (see cover *front*)
30-31 *background* (see **28-29** *background*) **31** (see **23** *T*).

CONTENTS

THE MOZART FAMILY

The Mozart family lived in Salzburg, Austria. There had been Mozarts living in the town for over a hundred years, since the days of David Mozart, Wolfgang's great-great-grandfather. David was a master mason, as were his sons. Wolfgang's grandfather, Johann Georg Mozart, was a bookbinder.

WOLFGANG'S FATHER

Wolfgang's father, Leopold, was a very respected composer. He also taught and played the violin and keyboard. He was especially interested in the violin and wrote an important teaching guide for this string instrument. This guide brought him fame throughout Europe.

▶ *Leopold Mozart (1719-1787), painted in 1765 when he was 46 years old.*

WOLFGANG'S MOTHER

Anna Maria Mozart was from a fairly well-to-do family. However, she was not musical or artistic and was poorly educated. In the Mozart family, Leopold made all the major decisions.

◄ *This portrait of Anna Maria Mozart (1720-1778) was painted two years after her death.*

— *A GENIUS IN THE MAKING* —
Wolfgang was lucky to have a composer for a father. Leopold wrote symphonies, concertos, chamber music, church music, songs and keyboard pieces.

A MUSICAL CITY

Although small, Salzburg was one of the most musical cities in Austria, and musicians from all over Europe were drawn to it. The city was controlled by the church and governed by the local Archbishop.

▲ *A picture of Salzburg, painted at the time when the Mozarts lived in the city.*

WOLFGANG IS BORN

Wolfgang Amadeus Mozart was born on 27 January 1756. He was the seventh and last child to be born in the family. However, only one other child survived infancy – a sister, Nannerl, who was four-and-a-half years older than Wolfgang.

WOLFGANG'S SISTER
Neither Nannerl nor Wolfgang had any formal schooling – they were taught by their father. Nannerl started music lessons when she was seven years old.

▶ *Nannerl Mozart (1751-1829), who, like her brother, was a gifted keyboard player.*

A GENIUS IN THE MAKING

At the age of three Wolfgang could already recognize patterns of notes on the keyboard. The piano became his favourite instrument. He wrote 28 sonatas for the piano and even a sonata for two pianos.

WOLFGANG'S BIRTHPLACE

The Mozart family rented the third floor of a house in Salzburg. The building looked out onto a square with a fountain in the middle. The house is still there today and is now a museum.

◄ *The Mozart Museum in Salzburg holds many pieces of Mozart memorabilia.*

HARPSICHORD

Wolfgang began music lessons when he was four. He started on the harpsichord, an instrument that looks like an old-fashioned piano. Unlike a piano, which hits the strings with small hammers, a harpsichord plucks the strings with quills.

► *The harpsichord was played as a solo instrument and to accompany singers and other instruments.*

THE YOUNG PERFORMER

On the evening of 24 January 1761, according to Leopold, Wolfgang learnt his first keyboard piece. A few months later, the young boy composed two pieces for the keyboard, which his father wrote down. Early the next year, Wolfgang and Nannerl formed a performing 'team' and started to tour the royal courts of Austria and Germany.

ROYAL COURTS

The children had never visited a royal court before, with its beautifully dressed gentlemen and ladies, uniformed servants and magnificent state rooms. However, they soon became used to these grand places.

▶ *Leopold wanted his children to impress the ladies and gentlemen of the royal courts of Europe.*

MUNICH

In January 1762, Leopold and the children travelled to Munich, Germany. This visit lasted three weeks, and it was Wolfgang and Nannerl's first trip away from home.

▼ *Maximilian Joseph III, who was Elector of Bavaria until 1777.*

▲ *A picture showing the centre of Munich at the time of the Mozarts' visit.*

MAXIMILIAN JOSEPH III

In Munich, the children played the harpsichord for the Elector, Maximilian Joseph III, who governed Bavaria in southern Germany. Electors were important rulers, almost like kings.

--- *A GENIUS IN THE MAKING* ---

Wolfgang had an amazing memory. At the age of 14, he wrote down the music, Miserere by the composer Gregorio Allegri, which he had just heard at a service in St Peter's cathedral in Rome – after only one hearing!

A Visit to Vienna

Leopold decided to take Wolfgang and Nannerl to the great Austrian capital of Vienna. The trip lasted over four months. The family stopped several times on the journey to give public concerts and play at the houses of the rich and noble.

Royal palace
Soon after arriving in Vienna, the children were invited to perform in front of the Empress of Austria at the royal palace of Schönbrunn.

◀ *The Schönbrunn Palace, Vienna, home of the Empress of Austria, Maria Theresa.*

A GENIUS IN THE MAKING
Wolfgang was not only a composer, but also earned his living as a keyboard player and violinist. He sang too, and wrote around 30 songs.

MARIA THERESA

As Empress of Austria, Maria Theresa was one of the most powerful women in Europe. She was also a singer and placed great importance on music and the arts.

▶ *Maria Theresa, who was Empress of Austria from 1740 until 1780.*

COURT CLOTHES

As a reward for their playing, Maria Theresa gave each of the children a set of 'court clothes'. Back in Salzburg, Leopold commissioned this painting of Wolfgang wearing his splendid new gift.

◀ *This portrait, painted in 1763, shows Wolfgang wearing his gift from the Empress.*

A GRAND TOUR

The trip to Vienna had been an enormous success. Because of this, Leopold gave up his regular musical activities in order to devote his time to promoting the children. He planned to take Wolfgang and Nannerl on a tour of Europe to visit some of its great cities.

▼ *Portrait of Leopold, Wolfgang and Nannerl Mozart painted in 1763.*

THE MOZARTS

Leopold commissioned this picture of himself and his family before they set off on their European tour. It's likely the painter made Wolfgang look much smaller than he was so he would seem even more amazing.

A GENIUS IN THE MAKING

Through constant travelling and performing as a child, Wolfgang learnt to compose very quickly. In 1788, he wrote three symphonies in only two months.

▲ *By today's standards, coach travel in Wolfgang's day was slow and tiring.*

COACH TRAVEL

Leopold especially wanted the children to perform in Paris and London, the two great musical centres of Europe. The family set off on their tour in their own carriage with a servant on 9 June 1763.

ORGAN PLAYING

One of the first towns they stopped in was Heidelburg in southern Germany. Wolfgang so impressed his audience with his organ playing that the church people had the organ inscribed with details of the great event.

▶ *The Mozarts arrived in the town of Heidelburg in July 1763.*

At the Court of Louis XV

On 18 November 1763, the Mozarts reached Paris, France. At first it seemed that the people of this great capital weren't interested in them. The letters of recommendation and introductions they had brought with them didn't seem to work. Finally, however, the invitations began to arrive.

◄ *The Palace of Versailles, home of the French king, lies just outside Paris.*

ROYAL SUMMONS

On New Year's Day, 1764, the children played before King Louis XV at the royal palace of Versailles. The king was so pleased with the children that he invited them to stay for two weeks.

A GENIUS IN THE MAKING

Wolfgang's first music was published in Paris – four sonatas for violin and piano. He dedicated two of these sonatas to Princess Victoire, one of the king's daughters.

A MUSICAL HOUSEHOLD

Louis ruled France from 1715-1774. His three daughters, the Princesses Adélaïde, Henriette and Victoire, were all musical and played string and keyboard instruments.

◄ *Louis XV came to the throne at the age of five and ruled until 1774.*

TO ENGLAND

The Mozarts set off for England on 10 April 1764. They were amazed by the English Channel – none of them had seen the sea before!

▼ *The white cliffs of Dover was the Mozarts' first view of England.*

PLAYING TO KING GEORGE

Reaching Dover, the party set off for London and presented themselves at the royal court. Leopold advertized the children as 'Miss Mozart of eleven and Master Mozart of seven years of age, prodigies of nature' – even though Nannerl was almost thirteen and Wolfgang was eight!

MUSICAL TESTS

King George amused himself by giving Wolfgang some musical tests. He made Wolfgang play music he hadn't seen before, accompany the singing of Queen Charlotte and make up a piece of music at the keyboard.

▲ *George III (1738-1820), the King of Britain.*

A GENIUS IN THE MAKING

Wolfgang composed his first symphonies in London during a period when Leopold was ill and the children were told to occupy themselves quietly. These symphonies were the first of 41 he wrote during his life.

A SPECIAL GIFT

Like the king, Queen Charlotte was very musical. In return for the welcome the royal couple gave to the Mozarts, Wolfgang wrote and dedicated six violin and piano sonatas to the Queen.

◀ *Queen Charlotte (1744-1818) was married to George III for more than 50 years.*

LONDON

Eighteenth-century London was a dirty, smelly place. But it was also a place of beautiful gardens, amazing architecture and grand streets. It was also an important European centre of music and culture.

▶ *A view of St Paul's cathedral towering over eighteenth-century London.*

HOME AGAIN

The stay in London was very profitable. After one successful concert, Leopold counted takings of over one hundred pounds, a huge sum of money in those days. It was now time to return home, with more concerts in cities along the way.

ILLNESS STRIKES

The family stopped in Antwerp, Belgium, where Wolfgang played the cathedral organ. However, the children fell ill with typhoid soon after, and the family was forced to pause for four months.

▶ *Antwerp cathedral, in the eighteenth century.*

A NEW SYMPHONY

After the children recovered, they spent four weeks in Amsterdam, Holland. Even though the children were still weak, they gave two concerts here.

◄ *Wolfgang's fifth symphony was performed for the first time in Amsterdam.*

PRINCELY SHOW

After leaving Amsterdam in the autumn of 1766, the Mozarts travelled back to Paris. Here, they were invited to play for the Prince de Conti at his palace.

► *Wolfgang performing for the Prince de Conti.*

─── *A GENIUS IN THE MAKING* ───

Wolfgang included the organ in much of his church music and wrote 17 organ sonatas. These sonatas were written to be performed during the speaking part of the church service.

THE OPERA COMPOSER

The family returned to Salzburg full of the sights and countries they had seen and the people they had met. They were soon off again, however, returning to Vienna, where Wolfgang was asked to write an opera. It was to be called *The Make-Believe Simpleton*. But when the piece was completed, no one wanted to perform it! Leopold suspected jealous rivals were to blame.

ARCHBISHOP SIGISMUND

Archbishop Sigismund was Leopold's employer in Salzburg. At first, he didn't believe the stories Leopold told about his son. So he locked Wolfgang in an empty room to see for himself if the boy really could compose – and the young composer proved that he could.

◄ *Archbishop Sigismund, who reigned from 1753-1771.*

MAGICAL OPERA

Wolfgang was only 12 years old when he wrote another opera, *Bastien and Bastienne*. It tells the story of a shepherd and shepherdess who are finally brought together by a magic spell.

◀ *Dr Mesmer hypnotizing a patient.*

▲ *The front page of the opera* Bastien and Bastienne.

DOCTOR ANTON MESMER

Anton Mesmer was a scientist, best known for his studies into hypnotism. He was also a good friend of the Mozarts. He built a private theatre on his grounds in Vienna, where he arranged for a performance of *Bastien and Bastienne*.

A GENIUS IN THE MAKING

It was not long before Wolfgang became well-known as an opera composer. His operas, such as The Magic Flute, *are still popular today and are performed regularly. Some musicians consider them the greatest operas ever written.*

THE CHILD CONDUCTOR

Overall, the return visit to Vienna wasn't very successful. The children were invited to the palace of Schönbrunn, but they were not asked to play and received no payment. But then Wolfgang was asked to compose music for the inauguration of a new church at the Orphanage in Vienna.

▲ *The Orphanage Church, where Wolfgang conducted his own music for the first time.*

ROYAL PRESENCE

The royal court of the Empress of Austria attended the concert at the new church in Vienna where Wolfgang's music was performed. The Mozarts left Vienna with their heads held high.

A GENIUS IN THE MAKING

Wolfgang was frequently called upon to write church music, which was sometimes performed at grand occasions. In 1791, one of his masses was performed at the coronation of the Emperor of Austria. It has been called the Coronation Mass *ever since.*

CONCERT MASTER

Back in Salzburg there was more good news – Wolfgang was made court 'concert master'. The job was unpaid, but it was a step in the right direction towards becoming a professional musician.

◀ *As court concert master, Wolfgang was in charge of the music for grand court events, such as this one.*

TRAVELLING AGAIN

On 13 December 1769, Leopold and Wolfgang set off for Italy, stopping off to give concerts along the way. As usual, Leopold kept a diary throughout the trip in which he recorded every detail of their travels and musical successes.

▼ *Innsbruck, Austria, where Wolfgang gave his first concert of this tour.*

A TRIP TO ITALY

Archbishop Sigismund had generously given Wolfgang 120 ducats towards his expenses in Italy. While on his travels, Wolfgang composed his first string quartet, some sacred music and symphonies. In Milan, he wrote a new opera, *Mithradates, King of Pontus*, and directed its first performance in December 1770.

A GOOD START

In Verona, Wolfgang's audiences went wild with delight for him. One music lover was so taken by Wolfgang's musical skills that he commissioned this picture of him!

▶ *Portrait of Wolfgang, aged 13, commissioned by a fan from Verona.*

─────── *A GENIUS IN THE MAKING* ───────
Wolfgang wrote a total of 20 string quartets.
He dedicated a set of six of these to the composer
Joseph Haydn, who greatly admired his work.

POMPEII

In the summer of 1770, the Mozarts visited the ruins of the ancient Roman town of Pompeii, which was then being newly excavated. Leopold considered sightseeing a very important part of his son's education.

◄ *The ruins of Pompeii, an ancient Roman town that was destroyed by a volcanic eruption.*

MEETING MUSICIANS

In Milan, the Mozarts were introduced to the best of society by the Austrian Governor General of the area. Leopold thought it was important for Wolfgang to meet 'everyone and everybody'.

◄ *The Italian composer Giovanni Battista Sammartini (c1700-1775) met the Mozarts in Milan.*

CONCERT MASTER

In March 1771, Leopold and Wolfgang returned to Salzburg after 15 months of travelling, bringing with them several commissions for new works. By the summer, however, they were back in Italy, where Wolfgang began work on a new opera.

ITALIAN OPERA

In Italy, the opera was a spectacular occasion, with lavish sets, beautiful costumes and excellent singing. Wolfgang learnt a lot from his visits to the opera, although one opera, *Armida* by Nicolò Jommelli, he described as a little 'old-fashioned'.

▶ *This lavish opera at the Teatro Argentina in Rome was typical of the performances that Wolfgang saw.*

A GENIUS IN THE MAKING

Wolfgang didn't usually choose what music he wrote. Instead, he was commissioned to compose for a fee. In 1790, a Viennese count even paid him to write music for a mechanical organ!

WEDDING MUSIC

Wolfgang was asked to write some of the music for the wedding of Princess Beatrice to Archduke Ferdinand, the son of Empress Maria Theresa. The wedding was a dazzling affair, and the audience called for Wolfgang's music to be repeated the following day.

◀ *Princess Beatrice was married in October 1771 and Wolfgang received a diamond-studded gold watch in payment for his music.*

PAID WORK

The day after their return to Salzburg, Archbishop Sigismund died. Luckily, his successor, Archbishop Colloredo, agreed to pay a wage for Wolfgang's position as concert master. It was his first paid appointment, at the age of just 16.

▶ *Archbishop Colloredo, who succeeded Archbishop Sigismund and reigned from 1771-1801.*

Wolfgang's Legacy

Now that Wolfgang had a permanent position, he imagined a successful career lay ahead of him. But it was not to be. He had financial problems throughout his life. He was often in debt and found it very difficult to find regular paid work. Instead, he earned money from commissions for his music and performing. But this income was not reliable.

Overwork

During his short life, Wolfgang was always overworked. Although he was able to compose quickly, his commissions were often only finished at the last minute. He would even improvise the piano solo during a concert if he had not been able to complete it in time.

▶ *Wolfgang as an adult, aged about 30.*

POOR HEALTH

As an adult, Wolfgang was often ill. It's likely that the pressures of touring as a young child permanently damaged his health and brought on an early death. In his lifetime, Wolfgang Amadeus Mozart wrote an enormous amount and range of music including symphonies, concertos, chamber and piano music, music for dance and ballet, operas, sacred music and songs. He died in Vienna on 5 December 1791, at the age of only 35.

▶ *This statue of Mozart was erected in the Mozartplatz in Salzburg on 4 September 1842.*

▼ *Mozart's signature*

A GENIUS IN THE MAKING

When the composer Joseph Haydn attended a concert in 1785, he described Wolfgang as 'the greatest composer known to me'.

GLOSSARY

BALLET MUSIC
Music written for dancers to perform to on the stage.

CHAMBER MUSIC
Music written for a small group of musicians.

COMMISSION
A paid request for a piece of music.

CONCERT
When players or singers perform in front of an audience.

CONCERTO
A piece usually for one instrument that is accompanied by an orchestra.

IMPROVISE
To make up the music at the same time as you play it.

KEYBOARD
Any instrument with notes, called keys, laid out as they are on a piano. Keyboards include harpsichords, pianos and organs.

MASS
The service of the Roman Catholic church set to music.

MUSICIAN
Someone who plays an instrument or sings.

OPERA
A musical play in which actors sing their parts.

ORCHESTRA
A large group of musicians.

PERFORM
To play or sing in front of other people.

SACRED MUSIC
Music that is written for church services.

SONATA
A piece of music that is made up of several sections called movements, usually for the piano or one instrument with piano.

STRING QUARTET
Music written for two violins, viola and cello to play together.

SYMPHONY
A long piece of music for an orchestra that is usually made up of four sections called movements.

INDEX